ideals
HOME
Vol. 50, No. 5

Publisher, Patricia A. Pingry
Editor, Tim Hamling
Art Director, Patrick McRae
Contributing Editors, Lansing Christman, Deana Deck, Russ Flint, Pamela Kennedy, Heidi King, Nancy Skarmeas
Editorial Assistant, Laura Matter

ISBN 0-8249-1110-5

IDEALS—Vol. 50, No. 5 August MCMXCIII IDEALS (ISSN 0019-137X) is published eight times a year: February, March, May, June, August, September, November, December by IDEALS PUBLISHING CORPORATION, P.O. Box 148000, Nashville, TN 37214. Second-class postage paid at Nashville, Tennessee and additional mailing offices. Copyright © MCMXCIII by IDEALS PUBLISHING CORPORATION. POSTMASTER: Send address changes to IDEALS, P.O. Box 148000, Nashville, TN 37214-8000. All rights reserved. Title IDEALS registered U.S. Patent Office.

SINGLE ISSUE—$4.95
ONE-YEAR SUBSCRIPTION—eight consecutive issues as published—$19.95
TWO-YEAR SUBSCRIPTION—sixteen consecutive issues as published—$35.95
Outside U.S.A., add $6.00 per subscription year for postage and handling.

ACKNOWLEDGMENTS

HOME by Edgar A. Guest from *JUST FOLKS*, copyright ©1917 by The Reilly & Britton Co. Used by permission of the author's estate. Our Sincere Thanks to the following authors whom we were unable to contact: Violet Rourke Broderick for SUNBEAMS; Anne Campbell for NEW ENGLAND HOUSES; Constance Cullingworth for NEIGHBORS; Bertha Kleinman for AT THE SIDE OF THE ROAD; T. L. Paine for HOME; Sheila Stinson for HOUSES ARE LIKE PEOPLE; Lucile Waer for SEAPORT TOWN; May Smith White for REMEMBERED YEARS; and Carice Williams for MY VILLAGE.

Four-color separations by Rayson Films, Inc., Waukesha, Wisconsin.

Printing by The Banta Company, Menasha, Wisconsin. Printed on Weyerhauser Husky.

The paper used in this publication meets the minimum requirements of American National Standard for Information Sciences—Permanence of Paper for Printed Library Materials, ANSI Z39.48-1984.

Unsolicited manuscripts will not be returned without a self-addressed stamped envelope.

Inside Covers   Cover Photo
John Walter   Gay Bumgarner

HOME TO ME

Agnes Davenport Bond

I have lived in stately halls
Where beauty was supreme,
Where, all about, the loveliness
Fulfilled a happy dream.

I have traveled many miles,
Have slept upon the sea,
When cradled by the rolling waves
That tossed incessantly.

I have camped in mountain wilds,
Nowhere to lay my head,
Except within a canvas tent
With pine boughs for a bed.

I have felt the desert winds
And breathed the desert air
And found within its loneliness
A kindred place to share.

I have loved these one and all,
Wherever they might be;
And if I had my loved ones near,
They all were home to me.

SUMMER RETREAT
Canandaigua, New York
Jim Schwabel
New England Stock Photo

A HOUSE THAT KNOWS

Edna Jaques

A house that knows the touch of trees
    Against the roof and on the walls,
A little lean-to at the back,
    Upon whose ridge the sunlight falls,
Who feels upon its portals wide
    The touch of those who live inside;

A house with windows bright and clear
    With scarlet flowers on the sill,
Where little fires softly glow
    To keep away the damp and chill,
Making a homey atmosphere
    Of quiet happiness and cheer;

A house that seems to show somehow
    The happy life within its walls,
Where laughter is a daily guest
    And little feet along the halls
Are busy running to and fro
    Like little puppets at a show;

Happy the house that holds within
    A little family of its own,
Where bonds of love and loyalty
    Are strong and safe as walls of stone,
Where Christian piety and grace
    Shed peace and joy upon the place.

SUMMER SHADE
Audubon Park, Kentucky
Adam Jones, Photographer

Home

T. L. Paine

God's mercy spread the sheltering roof;
　　Let faith make firm the floor;

May friend and stranger, all who come,
　　Find love within the door.

May peace enfold each sleeping place,
　　And health surround the board;

From all the lamps that light the halls
　　Be radiant joy outpoured.

Let kindness keep the hearth aglow
　　And through the windows shine;

Be Christlike living, on the walls,
　　The pattern and design.

THE COMFORTS OF HOME
Jessie Walker Associates

A Home

Margaret Rorke

Where two will toil together
    To make their human nest
Withstand life's windy weather
    And be a place of rest;

A center of affection,
    Where children love and learn
And find in retrospection
    The truths to which they turn;

A bond of interweaving
    The all that touches each,
A trust, a true believing,
    In everybody's reach;

A spell that's cast forever
    Upon the ones who roam;
For time and space can't sever
    The memory of a home.

PATRIOTIC HOME
Waterford, New York
Ed Cooper Photography

Someone There

Georgia B. Adams

Someone waiting on the threshold
As I walk my homeward way
Is the most I ask in return
For the labors of the day;

Someone there to bid me welcome,
One to smile, to lift, to share,

THE OPEN GATES OF HOME
Lewisburg, Pennsylvania
Jim Schwabel
New England Stock Photo

Just someone to really live for,
Someone there to love and care.

'Twixt the four walls of my homestead,
Just a cheery word or two
From a loved one is uplifting,
Helps to make the skies so blue.

So the most I ask in return
For the labors of the day
Is one standing on the threshold
As I walk my homeward way.

Houses Are Like People

Sheila Stinson

Houses are like people
Marching up and down
Streets and lanes and highways
Of countryside and town.

Some are new and shining,
Their yards all neat and clean;
Some have rows of fences
Built closely in between.

Some are tall and prosperous
And gaze with icy stare
When one that's small and simple
Invades their thoroughfare.

Houses are like people,
But doors must open wide
For one to hear the heartbeats
Of those who live inside.

New England Houses

Anne Campbell

New England houses hide their flowering gardens;
Their doorways open on the narrow street.
Knowing their secret loveliness, one pardons
The absent porch, the missing window seat.
For somewhere past their walls and high-board fences,
Far from the prying gaze of passersby,
A little dream of happiness commences,
A cool, green garden hugs its bit of sky.

New England houses are like love so treasured;
They cannot let the world know what's behind
The high, gray wall. Yet every day is measured
By love so deep it colors heart and mind.
Here is the sun-flecked pathway which arouses
The brooding will to wander and explore.
Here is the faith of old New England houses.
Here, peace abides behind an oaken door.

Seaport Town

Lucile Waer

You may have your prairie cities
Set in space that's broad and free;
I'll take a busy, bustling city
By the timeless, moving sea.

Some like a quiet mountain village
Sweet with scent of ferns and pine;
Give me any seaport town with
The sharp, clean smell of brine:

A seaport town where ships ply forth
To sail the seven seas, or find
A peaceful harbor, with voyage done,
And stormy dangers left behind.

Where sea gulls, white against the blue,
Soar in graceful, curving flight;
When darkness settles on the deep,
A ghostly fog creeps in at night.

A ship's deep-throated calling
Stirs the wanderlust in me;
I'm a stowaway in spirit
When ships put out to sea.

SEAPORT TOWN
Rockport, Maine
Fred Sieb Photography

50 YEARS AGO

The Call of New England

"Going home for Old Home Week this year?" It was one New Englander accosting another in a bustling Midwest metropolis.

"Never missed one yet!" came the laconic reply. "Can't drive, of course, but I'll get there some way, if I have to go by shank's mare!"

So strong is the pull of home! And it will be Old Home Week as usual this summer in those states that observe it. While the attendance will naturally be smaller, the joys of reunion should be deeper. Invitations have gone out from town and city to all wandering sons and daughters, stressing the need of "coming back to rest awhile from the struggle of the strenuous life of today." The soldier on the other side of the world, the sailor on the high seas, will think longingly of the old home town back among the hills; of his former playmates at the district school; of the white-spired church on the village green.

Nor are those serving the cause of their country forgotten in the festivities. Last summer the highlight of the celebration in some towns was the dedication of a service flag to the local boys in the armed forces.

For over 70 years some New Hampshire towns have been calling their "children" home each summer. However, it was not until 1899 that the custom received official sanction in that State when the Governor, Frank W. Rollins, designated the last week in August as Old Home Week. The response was instant and overwhelming, for more than 10,000 people returned to the haunts of their youth that first year. From as far away as California and Alaska they came; and many of them have been coming back each August since, without a break. In 1906 the New Hampshire Legislature enacted a law, authorizing the towns and cities of the State to vote money for Old Home Week purposes. A State association was formed, with local organization in the various communities.

Almost at once the idea caught on in other states; and Vermont, Maine, and Massachusetts each sponsored an official Old Home Week. And at least one town in Connecticut caught the spirit, starting first with an Old School Reunion which grew later into an Old School and Old Home Week. Thousands responded to the call; and the celebration has now been

The Old Neighborhood.

extended to cover Home, Church, School, and State. Gradually the sentiment spread still farther abroad—as far away as Ohio and Michigan. But it is to New England, and New Hampshire particularly, that the institution really belongs. It is as indigenous as doughnuts and pumpkin pie. During the seventies and eighties of the last century the population of the little hill towns drained away to the cities to an alarming degree; and New England was fast becoming a land of deserted farms. Sad, indeed, was it for those who were left; and the inspiration to bring back, even for a visit, those who had departed, renewed and strengthened the bond between them and the home folks. On their part, with a new perspective, the visitors saw that the old town needed and did something about it—often in a large-handed way.

For instance, half a dozen native sons were idly swapping reminiscences on the porch of a lakeside cottage. Someone remarked that the old church needed painting pretty bad. Within five minutes $100 was in "the hat" as their contribution to the cost! Another example of the Old-Home-Week spirit was noted in Vermont when a former resident, who had left home 50 years before, presented the town of his birth with a brand new town hall. Endowed libraries have sprung up in many places—perhaps one of the most far-reaching and worthwhile results of this mass return homeward.

Another deeply satisfying outcome has been the buying and restoring of those schoolhouses which they knew in days of yore. One group has formed a "Little Red Schoolhouse Association" to purchase and keep in repair for posterity its own old schoolhouse.

While the large cities celebrate the event in a more formal and pompous way, with big parades, band concerts, historical pageants, decorated buildings, speeches by the Governor of the state and native sons who have made their mark in the world, etc., the real essence of Old-Home-Week spirit is found in the little communities tucked away among the hills.

Last year some visitors came over the hills with horse and buggy; and this summer will doubtless see many more horses tethered in the old sheds back of the church—especially if the

The Familiar Streets of Home.

advice of a member of the State Association is followed. Said he, over the radio, "Old Home Week will help lift the spirit and morale of the people in your community this year as never before. Take a pair of horses and the hayrack, the carryall or buckboard, and bring the folks to Old Home Day."

The little town of Bedford, NH, sponsored a unique church service. Along the roads came the worshippers—in one-horse chaises, on saddle horses, even by oxcart. Further color was added by the costumes of their ancestors which they wore. As part of the service an old-fashioned choir sang the hymns of long ago. Time had indeed turned completely backward for one short hour.

One of the big New England dailies, in an editorial which appeared during Old Home Week, stated: "Outside of our public libraries, newspapers and schools, we doubt if any influence at work among us will produce better results for our people than Old Home Week."

Printed in The Christian Science Monitor, *July 31, 1943.*

19

The Road to Home

Ruth H. Underhill

There's a road that leads to the city,
    Where the people hurry along,
And one that leads to the country,
    Where the robin peals forth its song.

There's a trail that leads to a mountain,
    Lofty and towering high,
And one that leads to a valley
    'Neath a sparkling azure sky.

There's a path that leads to a woodland
    Near a cheerful babbling brook
And one that leads to an open field
    With golden grain as far as you look.

But of all the roads and trails and paths,
    No matter where they may roam,
The one I love is trampled and worn,
    'Tis the road that leads to home.

THE PATH TO HOME
Old Bennington, Vermont
Fred Sieb Photography

A SLICE OF LIFE

Edgar A. Guest

Home

The road to laughter beckons me,
    The road to all that's best;
The home road where I nightly see
    The castle of my rest;

The path where all is fine and fair,
    And little children run;
For love and joy are waiting there
    As soon as day is done.

There is no rich reward of fame
    That can compare with this:
At home I wear an honest name,
    My lips are fit to kiss.

At home I'm always brave and strong,
    And with the setting sun
They find no trace of shame or wrong
    In anything I've done.

There shine the eyes that only see
The good I've tried to do;
They think me what I'd like to be;
They know that I am true.

And whether I have lost my fight
Or whether I have won,
I find a faith that I've been right
As soon as day is done.

Edgar A. Guest began his illustrious career in 1895 at the age of fourteen when his work first appeared in the Detroit Free Press. *His column was syndicated in over 300 newspapers, and he became known as "The Poet of the People."*

At the Side of the Road

Bertha Kleinman

Let me come back to my little abode,
Back to my home
At the side of the road.
After the miles upon miles I've roamed,
Nothing so lovely as coming back home.
Greener her gardens and bluer her skies,
Friendlier, kindlier everyone's eyes,
Closer the handclasp
That lightens my load—
Let me come back to my humble abode.

Let me remain with the home folks I know,
Wishing Godspeed to
The ones who must go,
Busy and watching for those who must roam;
Nothing so lovely as coming back home.
Restless the throngs on
The highways without,
Wanderers often and bitter with doubt;
Let me remain in my humble abode,
Welcoming home at the side of the road.

A GARDEN'S SUMMER COLORS
Waldoboro, Maine
Dick Dietrich Photography

A Turn-of-the-Century Victorian Home.

Secret Cracks and Crevices

Melody Carlson

Grandma's tall Victorian house looked like a castle to me as a child. Proud and white, it roosted on a grassy knoll skirted by a colorful flower bed. Total strangers would pause to admire and even photograph Grandma's striking rock garden. The three-hour trip to Grandma's amounted to more than merely visiting her turreted home with its gingerbread trim and pretty flowers; it meant entering a world unlike my everyday one.

At Grandma's, everything changed, and I encountered a secret world—a world where only I knew all the fascinating nooks and crannies. I could dawdle away countless summer hours exploring its hidden corners. I remember the warm, earthy smell after a summer shower and the feel of the cool, damp cement through my thin cotton shorts as I sat on the steps behind Grandma's house. Lush, leafy fuchsia plants profuse with luxuriant purplish pink flowers overflowed the deep beds that bordered those steps. They looked like miniature Japanese lanterns, and the honeybees scurried about them gathering food. I remember the waxen feel of an unopened fuchsia blossom and the pop it made when pinched gently by my fingers—and the muffled, angry buzz of the unfortunate bee I imprisoned in the royal-colored depths of a bloom.

I would climb up those fuchsia-bordered steps to the home of Martha—Grandma's neighbor. Her flagstone patio, still wet from the rain, steamed and glistened in the afternoon sun. Beside her patio grew a small garden surrounded by a child-sized fence. I'd stand and lean my arms upon it and inspect the mysterious green foliage flourishing within. A long clothesline stretched high over the garden. On one end hung a pulley my grandpa had designed to draw the flapping white lines to and fro without having to set foot in Martha's garden. Martha and Grandma shared the line, dividing the sunshine between them.

Inside her sun-filled front room, Martha kept building blocks and wooden dolls, picture books and an old 3-D photo viewer—all for her young visitors. Of course, cookies and tea would invariably be served; it was a little girl's utopia.

An old and noble cherry tree grew in the narrow space between Grandma's house and Martha's. It was always dark and damp and sticky there, but it provided a cool refuge on a hot summer day. The almost-black cherries were as big as plums and burst ripe and sweet in my mouth. I delighted to see how far I could spew the pits, but my dark-stained lips and fingers always betrayed my cherry-tree escapades. Cherries have never been so big or sweet since then.

On the south side of the house lounged a sun-drenched patio and Grandma's well-known flower gardens. Black-eyed Susans, mums, roses, rhododendrons, and a rainbow of flora overflowed the beds contained by the high retaining wall, but my favorites were the pungent nasturtiums that spilled down the wall in splashes of orange and yellow. They even flourished between the cracks in the sidewalk—such brave and cheerful flowers—yet no one noticed or praised them like the other more dignified blooms. Silently, I'd venerate their sunny dispositions and make pleasant nosegays that looked more priceless than gold.

Down the street lived Grandma's sister, Londy. Londy's house reminded me of Snow White's cottage. Surrounded by towering trees and tucked in so neatly, it might have sprouted like an oversized mushroom. Londy, a tiny woman, fit flawlessly with her diminutive house. She liked to bustle about and prepare delectable snacks in her compact kitchen. She'd array toast and homemade preserves on flowery china for her much-welcomed guests, and she never discriminated between children and adults—we all ate from the same dainty dishes; no plastic was found in her kitchen.

Londy enjoyed cut flowers, and they often cascaded from the porcelain vases in her home. Outside her kitchen window grew roses, berry bushes, and mint. The mixture of their fragrances was almost intoxicating as it wafted in on a warm summer breeze. Londy's home felt like an enchanted, full-grown doll house.

We always stayed in the "barn" at Grandma's house. This wasn't an ordinary barn, but more like a dorm. The walls were covered with faded wallpaper decorated with huge, pink cabbage roses. My mom and my sister and I slept in the loft upstairs, like the Three Bears, in our three beds all in a row.

I'd be the first one up in the morning because I knew Grandpa had breakfast sizzling and steaming downstairs in the cozy kitchen. After eating, I'd linger at the table in front of the big picture window, where bright red geraniums bloomed year round in the window box. I'd try to spy the little green frog who lived in the geraniums and watch the hummingbirds flitter about the hanging flower baskets. Summers were timeless then—no schedule, no routine.

Although the places remain, the people are gone; and I'm torn between the desire to return and discover what time has done to my childhood paradise and the fear that the spell, now broken, would only bring disappointment. For the places I remember, even if they have remained unchanged, can never be found again because my child's eye perceived the hill as a mountain and the house as a castle. And so these memories must continue to endure in the secret places—hidden in the cracks and crevices—only to be visited through remembering.

Things That Never Die

Charles Dickens

The pure, the bright, the beautiful
That stirred our hearts in youth;
The impulses to wordless prayer,
The streams of love and truth;
The longing after something lost,
The spirit's yearning cry;
The striving after better hopes —
These things can never die.

The timid hand stretched forth to aid
A brother in his need;
A kindly word in grief's dark hour
That proves a friend indeed;
The plea for mercy softly breathed
When justice threatens high;
The sorrow of a contrite heart —
These things shall never die.

Let nothing pass, for every hand
Must find some work to do;
Lose not a chance to waken love;
Be firm and just and true;
So shall a light that cannot fade
Beam on thee from on high,
And angel voices say to thee —
"These things shall never die."

Sleeping on a Cloud

Bernice Maddux

While turning the mattress on my bed recently, I remembered how Mother used to rejuvenate the family's tired, well-worn mattresses when I was a child. At least twice a year she felt compelled to lug our unwieldy, homemade cotton mattresses out to the porch for a ritual comprised of a thorough beating, sunning, and airing.

She'd pick her day well in advance. As soon as the West Texas sun was well on its way across the sky, she would ask us kids to lend her a hand in wrestling the clumsy rectangles outdoors.

Then the beating began. Dust and lint scattered in all directions as Mother pounded both sides of a mattress with a clean broom. To our delight, if our feet were clean, she'd let us jump up and down on the mattresses while she rested for a few minutes. Then she banished us for several hours to let the mattresses bake under the scorching sun. Sometimes we'd sun them on our cellar door if the porch was needed for other activities.

About halfway through the day, we all marched back outdoors to help her turn the mattresses, flipping them over like giant pancakes that needed browning on both sides. When the sun began to go down and its rays and fresh air had worked their special magic, we wrestled the still-hot cargo of fluff back into the house. Mother then made the beds with fresh, clean sheets that had also dried in the sunshine and sweet summer air.

On those nights I actually looked forward to bedtime. As I crawled between the sheets, I could smell the wide-open outdoors and feel the warmth of the sun surrounding me. I'd drift off to sleep pretending I was sleeping on a cloud. Come to think of it, I was about as close as you can get.

Sunbeams

Violet Rourke Broderick

When the big, round sun is rising
On a lovely summer day,
He will gather all his little ones
So none will go astray.

And gently he will kiss them,
All these dancing, golden beams,
And send them off to waken
Little children deep in dreams.

32

These sunbeams will be merry
Through the hours of the day,
Playing hide-and-seek with shadows,
Chasing dark and gloom away,

They will brighten up a dim room
With a happy, friendly game,
Making pictures on the ceiling
That are lots of fun to name.

Changing morning dew to crystal,
Bringing rainbows to stained glass;
The baby's hair becomes spun gold
When a sunshine sprite skips past.

So whenever you are lonely
And there's nothing much to do,
Look about for little sunbeams,
The toys God made for you.

Country CHRONICLE

— Lansing Christman —

If there is a creek in the neighborhood, one that has a trickling flow in summer, it becomes a mecca for farm boys when their work in the blazing heat of day comes to an end. A deep pool at the base of a thirty-foot waterfall is their swimming hole, a place to seek the cool and soothing waters after long hours spent in the hot, dry fields. It is a pool of renewal, reviving the energy and spirits of the swimmers.

I went to such a place often as a farm boy, sometimes alone and sometimes with neighborhood friends. We went in late afternoon, daily sometimes, when the torrid heat of the August sun left shimmering waves dancing across the wide fields.

In later years, I began to think of the creek as a chronicler of the ages, probing into the very foundation of rock and stone that support the hills, prying deeper and deeper as the surging currents turned and tumbled stones in the bottom of the stream.

I learned to appreciate more profoundly the wildflowers growing along the creek—the mints and joe-pye weed, the cardinal flower and stitchwort. There were banks of woodbine and bittersweet and carpets of moss over the shelves of rock under which the phoebes built. Lush ferns thrived along the creek's bank.

It was along the stream that I found my first hummingbird nest, a miniature nest for a miniature bird built on the small branch of a tree high above the singing waters below.

Back in the woods, I found the nest of the ovenbird, a topped nest shaped somewhat like an oven. When I heard its song, it seemed to be calling "teacher-teacher-teacher" to me over and over again.

I found the nests of the veery and the vireo. On the ground I found the nest of a ruffled grouse and listened to the whir of its wings as it suddenly took flight, leaving a covering of dry brown leaves over the eggs. I often heard its rhythmic drumming throughout the woods.

I never walked the ravine or the woods without keeping a sharp lookout and a keen ear for the sights and sounds around me. It was my world of wonder, as is the world around me today in these later years. Wherever I go, the wonder is still there, in the woods or a creek's ravine, in a meadow or a field, in a swampland or in a pasture.

The author of two published books, Lansing Christman has been contributing to Ideals for over twenty years. Mr. Christman has also been published in several American, foreign, and braille anthologies. He lives in rural South Carolina.

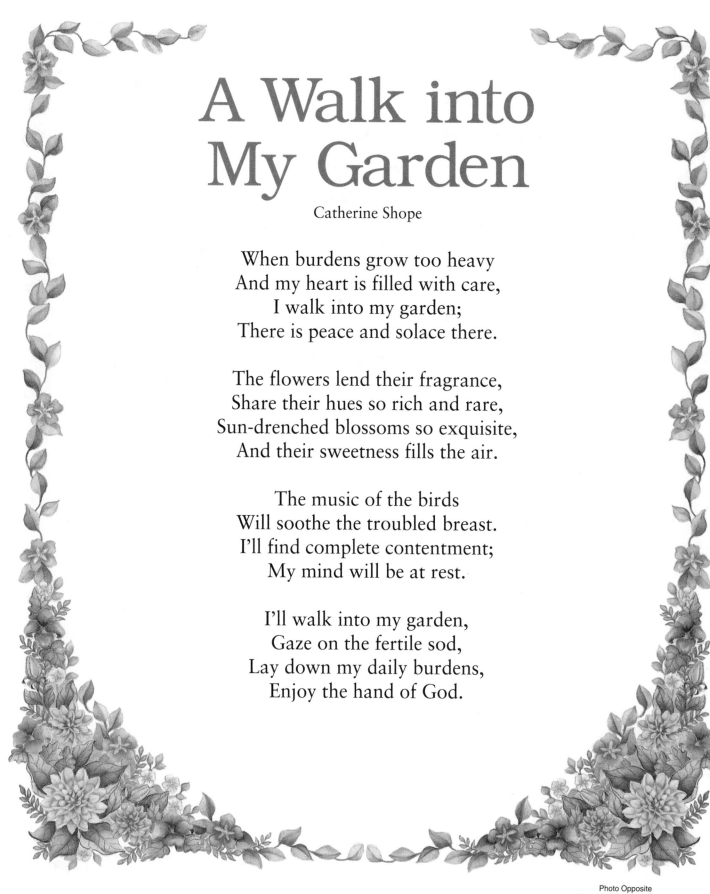

A Walk into My Garden

Catherine Shope

When burdens grow too heavy
And my heart is filled with care,
I walk into my garden;
There is peace and solace there.

The flowers lend their fragrance,
Share their hues so rich and rare,
Sun-drenched blossoms so exquisite,
And their sweetness fills the air.

The music of the birds
Will soothe the troubled breast.
I'll find complete contentment;
My mind will be at rest.

I'll walk into my garden,
Gaze on the fertile sod,
Lay down my daily burdens,
Enjoy the hand of God.

Photo Opposite
WISHING WELL AND GARDEN
Point Defiance Park, near Tacoma, Washington
Gay Bumgarner, Photographer

Ideals' Family Recipes

Favorite recipes from the *Ideals'* family of readers.

Editor's Note: If you would like us to consider your favorite recipe, please send a typed copy of the recipe along with your name and address to *Ideals* Magazine, ATTN: Recipes, P.O. Box 140300, Nashville, TN 37214-0300. We will pay $10 for each recipe used. Recipes cannot be returned.

CHOCOLATE MOLASSES PAN COOKIES

Preheat oven to 350°. Grease a 9 x 13-inch pan. In a saucepan, heat ½ cup of butter and ¼ cup of molasses. Add ¾ cup of brown sugar, firmly packed, and stir over low heat until sugar is melted. Remove from heat and let cool.

Beat 1 egg and add it to cooled molasses mixture. Sift together 1 cup of flour, ½ teaspoon of baking soda, and ½ teaspoon of salt. Add sifted ingredients to molasses mixture. Stir in 6 ounces of semi-sweet chocolate chips and mix well. Spread batter over bottom of greased pan. Bake in 350° oven for 20 minutes. Remove and cool pan on rack. Cut into bars.

Ruth Crockett
Midland, Michigan

PINEAPPLE NUT COOKIES

Preheat oven to 375°. In a mixing bowl, cream together 1½ cups of sugar and ½ cup of vegetable shortening. Add ½ cup of crushed pineapple, drained, and 2 eggs and mix well.

Sift together 3 cups of flour, 1 teaspoon of baking powder, ½ teaspoon of baking soda, and ½ teaspoon of salt. Add sifted ingredients to pineapple mixture. Stir in 1 cup of chopped walnuts and mix well. Drop by teaspoon onto a greased cookie sheet and bake in 375° oven for about 15 minutes. Makes 3 dozen.

Ithel Rook
Columbus, Ohio

OATMEAL SCOTCHIES

Preheat oven to 375°. In a mixing bowl, combine 2 cups of flour, 2 teaspoons of baking powder, 1 teaspoon of baking soda, and 1 teaspoon of salt. In a second mixing bowl, cream 1 cup of softened butter, 1½ cups of firmly packed brown sugar, 2 eggs, and 1 tablespoon of water. Add flour mixture to sugar mixture and mix well. Stir in 2 cups of butterscotch chips, 1½ cups of uncooked quick oats, 1 cup of chopped pecans, and ½ teaspoon of orange extract.

Drop by tablespoon onto greased cookie sheet. Bake in 375° oven for 10-12 minutes. Makes 4 dozen.

Barbara Bennett
Dayton, Ohio

GUMDROP COOKIES

Preheat oven to 350°. In a large mixing bowl, cream 1 cup of butter, 1 cup of sugar, 1 cup of brown sugar, firmly packed, and 2 eggs. Add 2 cups of rolled oats, 1 cup of coconut, 1 cup of gumdrops, cut in half, and 1 teaspoon of vanilla. Mix ingredients well.

Sift together 2 cups of flour, 1 teaspoon of baking powder, ½ teaspoon of baking soda, and a pinch of salt. Add sifted ingredients to rest of batter and mix well. Drop by teaspoon onto an ungreased cookie sheet and flatten out. Bake in 350° oven for 10-12 minutes until edges are brown. Makes 4 dozen.

Etta F. Miller
Edinburgh, Indiana

FROM MY
G·A·R·D·E·N
JOURNAL

Deana Deck

Green Bean Harvest, John Colwell, Grant Heilman Photography.

Bean Counters

When I was in the first grade, I had an encounter with a bean that was—to me at least—every bit as magical as the one Jack had with his fabled beanstalk. Our teacher asked us all to bring a jar of dirt to school. She gave us each a bean, which we planted in our jar next to the glass where we could see it. Wonder of wonders, it sprouted tiny roots, and then a little stem and leaf. In no time at all, it was a complete plant!

I do not remember what happened to my bean plant, but it doesn't matter; I'd had my first glimpse of the wonderful world of gardening, and I was hooked for life. To this day, nothing beats the thrill of waiting for those first seedlings to emerge from the warm, rich soil in early spring. Usually, some of the first plants to appear in my garden are the beans.

Beans are native American plants and, along with corn, squash, and melons, were major staples in the Native American diet long before European explorers set foot on the continent. The three basic types of beans are snap beans, shell beans, and dry beans, and all are easy to grow. Snap beans, also known as string beans, have edible pods. These beans are also called green beans, even though some are yellow and some are purple.

Snap beans are the first beans to ripen, but, since they require very warm soil—in the

40

sixty-five to seventy-five degree range—to germinate, they are not an early spring crop unless grown in a southern climate. They can, however, easily be started indoors in paper cups, or, as I learned in first grade, in a jar!

Snap beans will quit producing when they have produced a mature bean to propagate the species. To prolong the beans' harvest period, fool the plant by snipping off all the young beans before they reach maturity; the plant will produce a replacement within two or three days. The younger the bean, the more tender it is, so pick them when they are about a third of their mature size. If you wait until you can see the shape of the bean within the pod, you will have waited too long, and the bean will be tough.

Eventually, the bean will quit producing, so it is a good idea to plant snap beans successively about every two weeks in order to have a summer-long harvest. Check the average date of the first frost in your area and, keeping in mind the growth time of the variety you select, plant accordingly to avoid losing your last crop to frost.

Shell beans, which include lima and butter beans as well as black-eyed peas, can be eaten fresh or dried, but their pods are inedible. Limas and other shell beans require a longer growing season than snap beans, nearly three months of frost-free weather and warm soil, although some varieties can be grown in more northerly climates if started indoors. Shell beans should be picked when the pods are green, full-sized, and appear lumpy from the ripe beans inside.

Dry beans, which include kidney beans and navy beans, are allowed to dry out in the pod or on the plant before they are harvested and stored. Because they could be stored and transported very easily, dry beans were a major source of winter protein for early settlers and today are one of the better vegetable sources of protein available.

All three types of beans are available in either bush or pole form. Bush beans mature quicker but have a shorter harvest period and occupy more space in the garden. The pole bean, which can be grown vertically on single poles, tripods, or wire supports, are best for small gardens. They can even be grown in containers on patios and balconies. Pole bean varieties have a much longer harvest period and are more flavorful than bush varieties.

Beans must be planted in a sunny location, but they tolerate a wide range of soils and don't require much fertilizer because they can absorb nitrogen from the atmosphere and send it to their roots. Some beans do this so well that they are planted for this characteristic alone as a cover crop and are tilled under as green manure at the end of the season.

Beans can be stored in a variety of ways; they are easily "put by," as my grandmother used to say. Snap beans and shell beans can be canned or frozen, and shell beans can also be dried, either in the sun, as the pioneers did it, or in a one hundred forty-degree oven. Consider the beans two-thirds dry when they have lost half of their original weight.

Dry bean varieties are ready to store as soon as they are harvested; they just need a little cleaning. Dry bean plants are usually pulled up by the roots late in the season when the plant is dry and brown and the bean pods are hard. (You can test the beans by trying to bite one. If you can't, it's ready to harvest.)

If the plants are not quite dry and early frost or wet weather threatens, pull them up and hang them inside until they are completely dry. Then thresh the beans by whacking them against the side of a garbage can or other similar container or by putting them in a pillowcase or burlap or plastic bag and crushing the pods. After removing the plant stems, you can separate the beans from the chaff the same way Pocahontas, Priscilla Mullens, or Martha Washington did: on a windy day, pour them from a height of two or three feet onto a clean sheet or blanket. (Or use an electric fan as your source of wind to blow away the unwanted chaff.) Afterward, remove any damaged beans and store the good ones in clean, dry glass jars or airtight plastic containers to preserve for the upcoming fall and winter months. Be sure, however, to set some aside for immediate enjoyment as a reward for your summer labors.

Deana Deck lives in Nashville, Tennessee, where her garden column is a regular feature in The Tennessean.

SUMMER SUN

Robert Louis Stevenson

Great is the sun, and wide he goes
Through empty heaven without repose;
And in the blue and glowing days,
More thick than rain he showers his rays.

Though closer still the blinds we pull
To keep the shady parlour cool,

Yet he will find a chink or two
To slip his golden fingers through.

The dusty attic, spider-clad,
He, through the keyhole, maketh glad
And through the broken edge of tiles
Into the laddered hayloft smiles.

Meantime, his golden face around
He bares to all the garden ground
And sheds a warm and glittering look
Among the ivy's inmost nook.

Above the hills, along the blue,
Round the bright air with footing true,
To please the child, to paint the rose,
The gardener of the world, he goes.

The Singing Waves

Joy Belle Burgess

What are the wild waves singing
　　As they surge in from the sea?
What are their far-off whispers
　　And their moods of ecstasy?

What is their haunting message,
　　The sighing that I hear
As I watch the wild breakers
　　Come flowing ever near?

They rise and crest in beauty
　　In one triumphant roar
And pour their weight of glory
　　Upon the gleaming shore.

And lo, I run and frolic
　　In their waves of flying spray
And linger in the lacy spume
　　Before it ebbs away.

I feel at one with every wave
　　That sweeps upon the strand,
Where cool salt winds are blowing
　　O'er the shifting, silver sand.

I find a sweet enchantment
　　In the spell that holds me nigh,
The sea that soothes my every mood
　　With its tumult and its sigh.

I hear the wild waves singing
　　As they surge in from the sea,
And my heart runs out to meet them,
　　To know their ecstasy!

PORTLAND HEAD LIGHTHOUSE
Cape Elizabeth, Portland, Maine
Dianne Dietrich Leis, Photographer

BITS & PIECES

Our God, our help in ages past,
Our hope for years to come,
Our shelter from the stormy blast,
And our eternal home.

Isaac Watts

When home is ruled according to God's word, angels might be asked to stay with us, and they would not find themselves out of their element.

Charles Haddon Spurgeon

If this world affords true happiness, it is to be found in a home where love and confidence increase with the years, where the necessities of life come without severe strain, where luxuries enter only after their cost has been carefully considered.

A. Edward Newton

Many a man who pays rent all his life owns his own home; and many a family has successfully saved for a home only to find itself with nothing but a house.

Bruce Barton

The beauty of the house is order;
The blessing of the house is contentment;
The glory of the house is hospitality;
The crown of the house is godliness.

Author Unknown

He is the happiest,
be he king or peasant,
who finds peace in his home.

Goethe

Here sparrows build upon the trees
 And stock dove hides her nest;
The leaves are winnowed by the breeze
 Into a calmer rest:
The blackcap's song was very sweet,
 That used the rose to kiss;
It made the Paradise complete:
 My early home was this.

John Clare

47

My Town

Lucille McBroom Crumley

My town is made of simple things like these:
Green lawns, gay flowers, and maple trees.
Some stores, a school, three churches stand
To hold us tightly in one hand.
All the love I knew was there;
I never yearned to go elsewhere.

I never found a golden touch,
But, oh, of life, I learned so much.
I love that town where children play,
And I often stop to pass the day
Where I am queen of all I own,
Friends for my subjects and love for my throne.

Photo Opposite
THE STREETS OF HOME
Original Painting by George Hinke

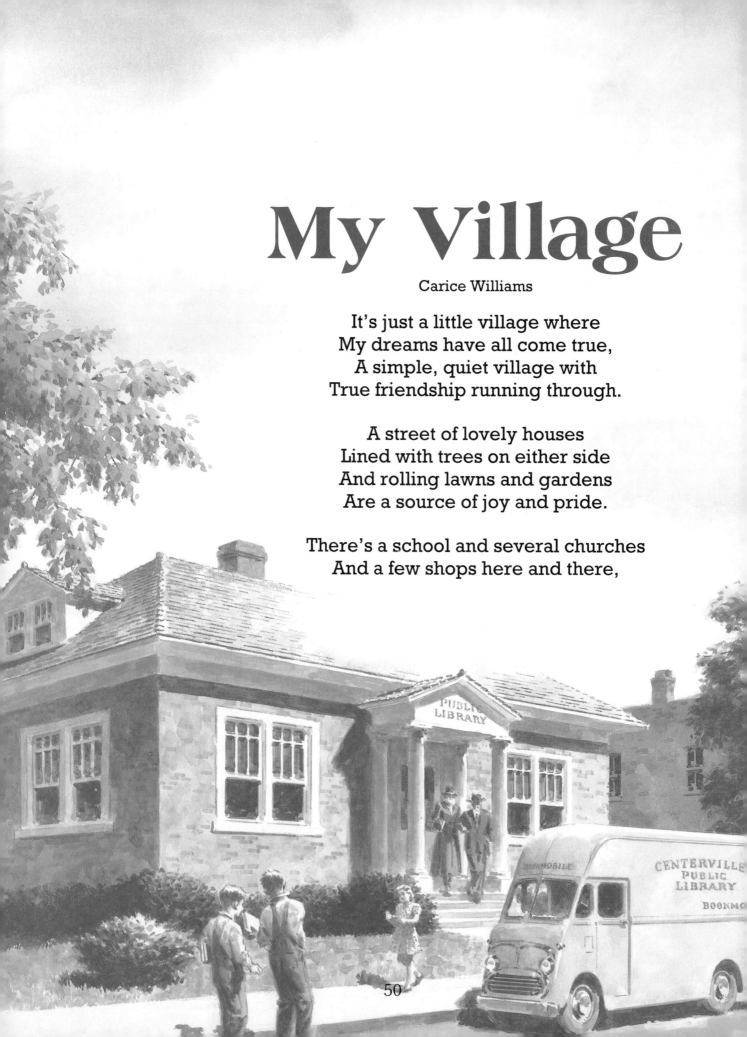

My Village

Carice Williams

It's just a little village where
My dreams have all come true,
A simple, quiet village with
True friendship running through.

A street of lovely houses
Lined with trees on either side
And rolling lawns and gardens
Are a source of joy and pride.

There's a school and several churches
And a few shops here and there,

And the town hall with its tower
Standing in the village square.

Oh, there's warmth and happy living
In this village old and sweet;
There is peace and quiet comfort
That you'll find real hard to beat.

No wonder when I'm traveling far,
For this dear place I yearn;
Though cities fair may beckon me,
It's here I still return,

Where there is no need to hurry
And the air is calm and clear,
To this little, quiet village
That my heart holds ever dear.

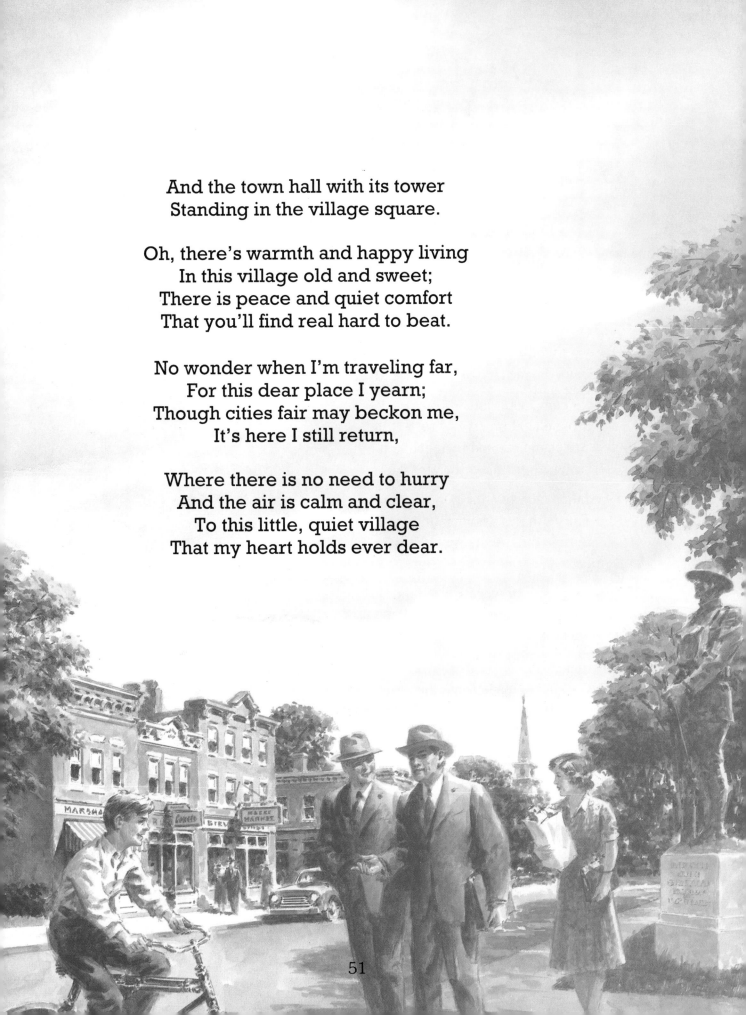

FOR THE CHILDREN
ARTWORK BY RUSS FLINT

A Sudden Shower

James Whitcomb Riley

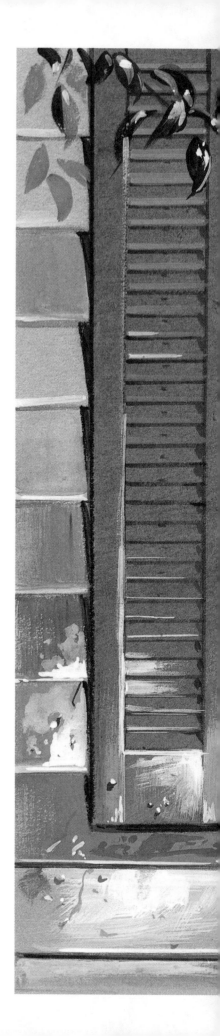

Barefooted boys scud up the street
    Or scurry under sheltering sheds;
    And school-girl faces, pale and sweet,
Gleam from the shawls about their heads.

Doors bang, and mother-voices call
    From alien homes; and rusty gates
    Are slammed; and high above it all,
The thunder grim reverberates.

And then, abrupt—the rain! the rain!—
    The earth lies gasping; and the eyes
    Behind the streaming windowpane
Smile at the trouble of the skies.

The highway smokes; sharp echoes ring;
    The cattle bawl and cowbells clank;
    And into town comes galloping
The farmer's horse with steaming flank.

The swallow dips beneath the caves
    And flirts his plumes and folds his wings;
    And under the Catawba leaves
The caterpillar curls and clings.

The bumblebee is pelted down
    The wet stem of the hollyhock;
    And sullenly, in spattered brown,
The cricket leaps the garden walk.

Within, the baby claps his hands
    And crows with rapture strange and vague;
    Without, beneath the rose bush, stands
A dripping rooster on one leg.

Readers' Reflections

Editor's Note: Readers are invited to submit unpublished, original poetry for possible publication in future issues of *Ideals*. Please send copies only; manuscripts will not be returned. Writers receive $10 for each published submission. Send material to "Readers' Reflections," Ideals Publishing Corporation, P.O. Box 140300, Nashville, TN 37214-0300.

Garden Gifts

Red, red, crimson, red
    Upon the trellis white;
Crowns and buds of roses
    Are such a lovely sight.

The songbirds come to sing
    In rose trees by the pool;
There waxen lilies float
    In water clear and cool.

In shady corner nooks,
    The lacy ferns stand tall;
Purple irises dance
    Along the garden wall.

Honeysuckle vines
    A-buzz with honeybees;
Periwinkle creeping
    Beneath the willow trees.

On green and stately stems,
    Jack-in-the-pulpits nod,
Ready for their sermon,
    "Flowers are gifts from God!"

Mary Masten Kimmel
Surprise, Arizona

My Lane

I long to live at the end of a lane,
At the top of a windswept hill,
Away from the world of greed and gain,
Where all is peaceful and still,
Away from the busy marts of men,
Where the waves of traffic beat;
Just let me live at the end of my lane
In a peaceful, quiet retreat,
Atop a hill, close to the sod,
In solitude and silence, the whispers of God.

Oa Haycook
Bradenton, Florida

Porch Music

Wind chimes on gentle breezes
Sound softly in the night.
They bid me close my eyes;
They put my fears to flight.

I hear their tinkling tones and
Know from whence they come:
There, on my neighbor's porch,
Wind chimes send a welcome.

They live next door; my friends,
They keep an eye on me.
Melodic chimes define
My friends as neighborly.

So when I seek my bed
And turn out every light,
I feel safe, reassured,
By porch chimes in the night.

Gene Ash
Lancaster, Ohio

God Bless This Home

Bert Whitehouse

God bless this home in which we live;
    God bless its every part.
God grant it peace and sweet content;
    God grace our every heart.

God bless each portal of this home;
    Let friendship light each way.
Let loving, kindred fellowship
    Be ours herein, we pray.

God bless each soul that enters in
    And bless him on his way.
God enter in this home of ours
    And bless it every day.

A WELCOMING HOME
Millbridge, Maine
Dick Dietrich Photography

Home

I was asked to tell a little about my home the other day when some friends gathered to become better acquainted. The request was innocent enough, but it set me thinking. When a person has lived, as I have, in sixteen different houses in the past twenty-three years, where or what exactly does one call home?

Our very first home was a tiny one-bedroom, furnished apartment located in Auburn, Washington. It was officially labeled "efficient" by the landlord who had obviously never lived there. The tiny kitchen had an oven and a dishwasher located directly across from one another, which meant I could never open both appliances at the same time because the doors would hit.

Despite the apartment's size, our heating bills were hefty due to the brisk breezes that continually swept in under the doors and around the window frames. The furnishings in our first home had been enjoyed by many previous tenants, and several pieces showed wear, including the bed, which gave way with a mighty crash one morning as my husband sat down to tie his shoes. Although we lived in it for only six months, this first home provided a wealth of anecdotes and memories.

As we moved around the country at the inscrutable whims of the navy, we lived in a variety of houses. Some were larger than others, but each was unique. There was a duplex on a naval base in Hawaii that came equipped with its own menagerie. In addition to the rats racing between the walls, a family of mice regularly ventured into our living quarters, large brown water bugs dashed to and fro, and several chameleon-like geckos chirped and winked at us from the tops of doors and the backs of cupboards. I was amazed how quickly we all adjusted to our island friends and could not understand the tense expressions of our houseguests visiting from the mainland.

While stationed in the Midwest on recruiting duty, we lived in an eighty-year-old bungalow near Milwaukee. It had been remodeled by the previous owner who must have hit a fire sale on hot pink and gold-plated bathroom fixtures. It was a decorating challenge that we met with the same philosophy that helped us through other housing dilemmas: "Well, we won't be living here for long!"

During one short stint in Newport, Rhode Island, we rented a bed and breakfast during the off-season. For once we had lots of space, but I could never find any of the kids when I needed a hand! The house had started out as one three-bedroom home but had sprouted additions like afterthoughts; there was just no rhyme or reason to the floor plan. When someone came to the door, we all dashed around hoping to catch him before he left since there were two front doors and two back doors and all the doorbells sounded the same! It was a crazy place to live, but it offered us one of our more memorable Christmases when we finally had enough bedrooms for my husband's family to spend a week with us.

A second tour in Hawaii landed our family on Ford Island, a tiny community accessible only by ferry in the middle of Pearl Harbor. Our spacious quarters were shaded by banyans and palms, caressed by soft trade winds, and surrounded by spacious green lawns. It was a historical setting, located behind the SS *Arizona* Memorial, and we enjoyed its tropical tranquility for three lovely years.

Now we are back on the East Coast, living in a traditional two-story brick home in a well-established neighborhood. There are leaves to rake in the fall and bulbs that bloom in the spring. We have country-print cushions on our Hawaiian rattan furniture and bathroom fixtures in conservative shades of white and blue. I've seen nothing more disturbing than a wayward cricket in the family room, and when the fire is burning and the cat is purring on the hearth, I feel I am at home.

The problem is, I feel equally at home under California palms, Hawaiian banyans, Rhode Island firs, and Virginia magnolias. Perhaps it is because to me home is not so much a function of where you live but of how you live. It is defined not by floor plans or even street maps, but by the places in your heart where memories, both sad and happy, have come to rest.

Pamela Kennedy is a free-lance writer of short stories, articles, essays, and children's books. Married to a naval officer and mother of three children, she has made her home on both U.S. coasts and in Hawaii and currently resides in Washington, D.C. She draws her material from her own experiences and memories, adding bits of her imagination to create a story or mood.

Home

Garnett Ann Schultz

There seems to be a magic truth
Within that one word *home*.
The comforts there are still the best
A heart has ever known,
Where understanding thoughts do dwell
And hope and love abide,
A hallowed spot where dreams are sweet
And laughter lives inside.

'Tis here we find a tenderness,
A mother-love so fine;
The wondrous peace of sweet content,
So surely yours and mine;
A quiet from the winter storm,
A roof to keep out rain;
The warmth of love we ever share,
The joy of spring again.

Where children play and kindness is
The strength of faith to share
The memories we know and keep
Whether skies are gray or fair,
'Tis built on love and filled with dreams
Where no one walks alone;
For God so surely dwells within
The truly happy home.

LEGENDARY AMERICANS

Peggy Schaefer

Isabella Stewart Gardner

At a time when women were valued more for their appearances and social graces than for their intellects, Isabella Stewart Gardner was intelligent, free-thinking, and independent in manner—a woman determined to live as she pleased. Her interests ranged from philosophy to baseball, and her generosity benefitted a wide range of charities, including the Boston Symphony, the New England Home for Little Wanderers, and the Birds of Massachusetts Fund.

She is best known for her patronage of the arts and for the Isabella Stewart Gardner Museum in Boston, which she began constructing in 1899.

Born in New York City on April 14, 1840, Isabella Stewart was the daughter of David Stewart and Adelia Smith, whose ancestors could be traced back many hundreds of years in Scottish and English history respectively. She married John Lowell Gardner in 1860, and the couple quickly established themselves in Boston society.

A son, John L. Gardner III, died at the young age of twenty months in 1865, and Mrs. Gardner's subsequent depression prompted Mr. Gardner to take his wife to Europe for recuperative reasons.

Mrs. Gardner returned with her spirits restored and a new passion for life. With an exuberant wit and an "as I please" attitude, Mrs. Gardner captured the admiration of much of Boston society. While some of the women felt she had crossed the line of decorum for a woman of her time, the men were almost unanimously captivated by her spirit. Much as she later acquired her art collection, Mrs. Gardner surrounded herself with what she considered the best of society—the best polo player to cheer, the best tenor to listen to, the best dancer to partner with, the best art critics to turn to for advice.

Later trips to Europe, mainly beginning in 1874, sparked the beginnings of the Gardners' art collection. Having already acquired some minor works of art in 1888 in Seville, Mrs. Gardner purchased her first old master, a Madonna by Francisco de Zurbarán. To this day, it hangs in the museum's Spanish Chapel. Mrs. Gardner's interest in art grew, and after receiving a $1.6 million inheritance upon her father's death in 1891, she began collecting in earnest.

In 1898, John Gardner's death left Mrs. Gardner control of the estate. Mrs. Gardner immediately immersed herself in bringing to fruition the museum they had envisioned together. She purchased the land for Fenway Court, as she called the museum, just weeks after her husband's death and soon left for Europe to seek architectural elements, such as columns, fireplaces, and arches, which she hoped to integrate into the building. Construction began in 1899, and Mrs. Gardner was on site every day to oversee and modify the design of the structure as she saw fit. The building, which resembles a fifteenth-century Venetian palace, was completed in December 1901. Today, the museum boasts more than two thousand pieces, including paintings, sculptures, prints, furniture, textiles, ceramics, and glass.

Among the many character traits which secured Isabella Stewart Gardner's place in society were her love of the arts and her patronage of its many members. Music played nearly as important a role in the creation of Fenway Court as visual art. In fact, on opening night, New Year's Night, 1903, guests were treated to a concert of Bach, Mozart, Chausson, and Schumann played by members of the Boston Symphony. Later visitors to the museum included such notable musical talents as Paderewski, Nellie Melba, and Arthur Rubenstein; but her patronage extended beyond the famous to include concerts benefitting the Manuscript Club, an organization which promoted the works of young local composers.

Mrs. Gardner was equally generous in her support of painters, sculptors, and writers. Of particular note was her friendship with Bernard Berenson, whom she met while attending an art history lecture at Harvard. So impressed was she with his brilliance, that she contributed to a traveling fellowship for Berenson that allowed him to study in Europe. Berenson became recognized as an expert on Renaissance art, and his advice proved invaluable to Mrs. Gardner as she continued to add to her collection. Apparently the admiration was mutual, for Berenson wrote of Mrs. Gardner: "She is the one and only real potentate I have ever known. She lives at a rate and intensity and with a reality that makes other lives seem pale, thin, and shadowy."

Not long after Christmas, 1919, Mrs. Gardner suffered a stroke which left her partially paralyzed. Although she did not walk again, Mrs. Gardner never lost her vivacious spirit. She wrote to an old friend in 1922:

> I'm quite an invalid but cheerful to the last degree. . . . I keep up a lot of thinking, and am really very much alive. . . . I have music, and both young and old friends. The appropriately old are too old—they seem to have given up the world. Not so I, and I even shove some of the young ones rather close.

Isabella Stewart Gardner died on July 17, 1924, leaving her museum and a $3.7 million endowment toward its upkeep as her legacy. Her final action, like all her others, reflected the motto she inscribed on the museum's shield: *C'est mon plaisir* (It is my pleasure.).

TRAVELER'S Diary

Peggy Schaefer

The Courtyard of the Isabella Stewart Gardner Museum.
Photograph courtesy of the Isabella Stewart Gardner Museum.

Isabella Stewart Gardner Museum

Boasting more than two thousand objects encompassing three thousand years and numerous cultures, the Isabella Stewart Gardner Museum in Boston includes paintings, sculptures, prints, furniture, textiles, ceramics, and glass. The museum is designed in the style of a fifteenth-century Venetian palace, with some elements, such as window frames and balconies, actually imported from Venice. Public galleries on the museum's first three floors open onto a central courtyard, which is always filled with

flowering plants and trees. The fourth floor served as Mrs. Gardner's home until her death in 1924. The museum's design won its architect, Willard T. Sears, a gold medal from the Philadelphia Society of Architects. Sears is said to have noted, however, that because of her significant contribution to the design and construction of the building, the award should rightly have gone to Mrs. Gardner.

The arrangement of the collection reflects Mrs. Gardner's belief that art should be displayed in such a way as to fuel the observer's imagination. Objects are not placed in chronological order, nor according to their country of origin or their importance in the world of art. They are specifically placed to enhance the beauty of each piece. In many cases, they remain unlabeled in order to encourage visitors to react to the object rather than the creator or title of the object. Thus, the arrangement creates an overall impression that is both soothing and inspiring.

The sole creation of Isabella Stewart Gardner, Fenway Court, as she called the museum, is the only private collection in which both the art and the building housing the art are the creation of one individual. At the time of their purchase of Rembrandt's *Self-Portrait* in 1896, Mrs. Gardner and her husband, John, envisioned a museum to house their increasingly important art collection.

Today, the museum contains some of the world's most important pieces of art. Masterpieces by Titian, a polyptych by Simone Martini, and a fresco by Pierra della Francesca are some of the more significant Italian Renaissance pieces in this country. A variety of sculptures, including Greco-Roman marbles, medieval wood figures, and bronze busts, are placed throughout the museum's three floors. Additional paintings by Botticelli, Raphael, Vermeer, Degas, Matisse, John Singer Sargent, and James McNeill Whistler attest to the museum's eclectic design. Period furniture, tapestries, ceramics, stained glass, and metal work are interspersed with the other artwork to ensure that no corner of the museum would be unadorned.

Mrs. Gardner acquired much of the collection herself, although she did look to John Singer Sargent and Henry Adams for advice on paintings, furniture, stained glass, and textiles. Bernard Berenson, an authority on Renaissance paintings, became an influential advisor on the purchase of European paintings and Oriental art. The museum collection also includes rare books and correspondence from such notables as Henry Adams, T. S. Eliot, Sarah Bernhardt, and Oliver Wendell Holmes; and many consider the architectural elements of the building to be valuable pieces of art history.

Designed by Mrs. Gardner, Fenway Court's construction began in 1899 and was completed in December 1901. During that time, she was on site every day to supervise the construction, including the installation of the architectural elements she and her husband had brought back from their earlier visits to Europe.

While friends and family enjoyed a sneak preview following midnight mass on Christmas Eve in 1901, the official grand opening of the Gardner Museum took place on New Year's Night, 1903—and grand it was. Guests listened to a concert of Bach, Mozart, Chausson, and Schumann performed by members of the Boston Symphony Orchestra. Later the doors were opened to give the guests their first view of the courtyard—a spectacular display of flowering plants and lantern lights.

Although Mrs. Gardner lived on the museum's fourth floor, she opened Fenway Court's doors and collections to the public and became an important part of Boston's culture. Mrs. Gardner frequently entertained in the galleries of Fenway Court, and her dinner guests included Julia Ward Howe, Henry James, Nellie Melba, and John Singer Sargent. Fenway Court also hosted local musicians and European visitors alike. Many concerts were held at the museum, and the many charities Mrs. Gardner favored often benefitted from these events. Even today, the museum offers over one hundred concerts a year to the public.

With a collection that includes paintings by master painters from numerous periods and countries as well as fine sculptures, metal work, ceramics, books, prints, and drawings, Isabella Stewart Gardner surely achieved what she described as her life work:

> Years ago, I decided that the greatest need in our country was art. We were largely developing the other sides. We were a very young country and had very few opportunities of seeing beautiful things, works of art. . . . So I determined to make it my life work if I could. Therefore, ever since my parents died, I have spent every cent I inherited . . . in bringing about the object of my life.

Handmade Heirloom

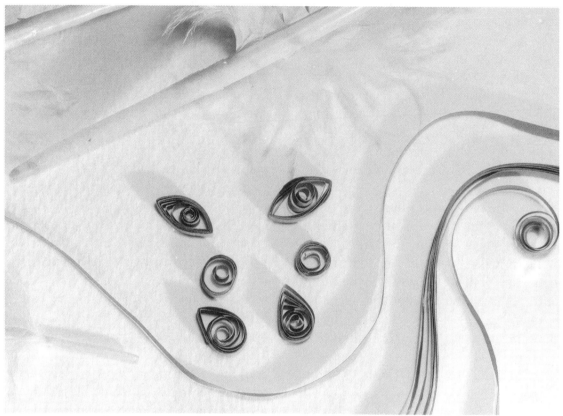

Three basic shapes for quillwork: the diamond, the coil, and the teardrop. Photograph by Robert Schwalb.

Quillwork

Heidi King

As far back as the thirteenth and fourteenth centuries, a lavishly decorated item was perceived by many to have more value than one with a simple design. Consequently, artisans used filigree—an ornamental openwork design in which gold, silver, and copper wires, or sometimes beads, are intricately shaped to decorate a wide variety of surfaces—to embellish items ranging from French wrought iron to portrait frames and jewelry. Filigree, however, was neither cheap nor easy to execute since nearly all the works were carved in stone and ivory or shaped from gold and silver. Inevitably, an alternative form of handiwork needed to be created for more widespread use, and quillwork—delicate, rolled paper designs

66

that imitated filigree—soon appeared.

It is unknown when the craft of rolling paper came into existence. Since paper was not as abundant as it is today, most historians conclude that quillwork began as thrifty book manufacturers saved the trimmings cut from the long edge of each page. The thin, narrow trimmings could be rolled and curled around the quill of a bird's feather. When gilded in rich colors or gold and silver, the paper amazingly appeared to be created from metal. When painted white, the coils resembled expensive ivory filigree. These deceiving paper imitations were named scrollwork or quillwork because of the utensils used to create the intricate pieces.

In the seventeenth century, Italian nuns perfected this craft as they created intricate designs from clusters of coils rolled in various sizes and shapes to produce stunning pieces of religious art. Quillwork filled a great need during this time since devoted members of the church felt that symbols of faith should be embellished as lavishly as possible. The art quickly spread to France and Spain, where frames, crosses, and medallions were only a few of the many items produced.

Quillworkers often painted their paper in vibrant colors or painted just the edges in gold to be used exclusively in quillwork. Some historians believe that many seventeenth-century manuscripts had pages intentionally cut one-eighth inch shorter to provide gilded strips for zealous quillers.

Late in the century, quilling became fashionable among members of the royal court and England's elite. By 1700, tutors were even available to teach the craft. Quillwork was no longer limited to religious articles; no object was too great or too small to embellish with the delicate coils. Quillwork covered tea trays and vanities,

elaborate quilled borders framed needlework, and quilled mosaics patterned after famous designs decorated cabinets. Magazines from the era even provided instructions and patterns.

During the next century, American quillers elevated the craft to a higher level by creating quilled compositions that included dried flowers, painted medallions, wax figures, pinecones, shells, feathers, beads, paper edged with wire, and sparkling mica flakes. Sconces, shadow boxes covered with glass, and candle brackets were popularly decorated items.

Today, quilling is easier than ever. While many of the techniques remain the same as those used in previous centuries, the supplies needed are readily available. Paper can be purchased in one-eighth-inch wide strips in an assortment of colors; and, instead of using a quill, many crafters now rely on a hatpin or wooden toothpick to coil the tiny rolls. While the work is easy to execute, most intricate designs can be time-consuming to complete.

Regardless of how complicated a quillwork piece might appear, all patterns are formed from simple variations of a few basic coils and scrolls. Grouping several coils and scrolls on a piece of wax paper and then gluing the paper coils together along the sides creates a lavish effect. For interesting shapes, such as hearts, diamonds, or tear drops, the coils are delicately pinched in one or more places to crease the paper and retain the shape. When a crafter does commit to learning this age-old technique, the result is delicate, spiral-shaped designs as ornate as the filigree that inspired it.

Heidi King makes her home in Tallahassee, Florida, and loves all arts and crafts.

COLLECTOR'S CORNER

Tim Hamling

Copper Fire Engine, Shelburne Museum, Shelburne, Vermont. Photograph by Ken Burris.

Weather Vanes

A rich history, tremendous variety, and fine craftsmanship—all these factors explain why weather vanes have become one of today's more popular collectibles. From the weather vane's earliest ancestor—an image of the Greek god Triton, dating back to 48 B.C., displayed on the Tower of Winds in Athens—the craft has evolved into an art form with both decorative and functional purposes.

The weather vanes decorating today's rooftops owe their existence to medieval Europe. European churches topped their bell towers with weathercocks, a symbol of vigilance; and European noblemen flew fanes, metal-supported banners displaying the family's coat of arms, over their castles. Over the years, the two emblems combined to create the term "weather vane," and the traditional symbols began to appear in America as European immigrants moved to this country.

Early American weather vanes adorned churches and community buildings, but they were soon found atop houses, barns, and business establishments. The weathercock remained a popular design, but other figures soon appeared as Americans discovered a second purpose for the vanes. In addition to pointing into the wind to indicate its source, weather vanes became one of the first forms of advertising. Individuals and businesses had specific figures crafted to symbolize their trade: fish for fishermen, cattle and sheep for livestock farmers, a quill for lawyers, a boot for cobblers, and nearly anything else that an individual requested.

Although some early vanes were carved from wood, skilled metalworkers and blacksmiths crafted many early vanes from sheet iron and copper. When viewed closely, these shapes often appear out of proportion; but these irregularities enable the vane to be viewed accurately from a distance as it sits perched atop its mount. Some vanes were flat silhouettes cut from metal, but elaborate designs were soon constructed using wooden models over which copper could be hammered to create a hollow, three-dimensional shape. These wooden models led the way to iron molds that could be used over and over to make the same design.

By the mid-nineteenth century, weather vane manufacturers had emerged using these molds to produce vanes at higher volume and lower cost than individual metalworkers could. Weather vanes became a popular addition to the decorative adornment gracing the period's Victorian architecture. A wealth of new designs—mermaids, locomotives, fire engines, ships, and steamboats—appeared at prices ranging from fifteen to four hundred dollars; but the traditional designs, roosters and other animals, remained the most popular.

The manufacture of weather vanes declined in the early decades of the twentieth century, but their popularity did not. Old vanes were repaired, and new ones were made, this time by individual artisans capitalizing on the increasing interest in folk art.

The popularity of weather vanes makes them a popular collectible, though one that is easier to acquire for sentimental and decorative value than for investment. The most valuable weather vanes are those that can be attributed to a specific blacksmith or manufacturer and can be priced at thousands of dollars—certainly out of most collectors' price ranges. In addition to these daunting prices, it is difficult to verify a vane's date and authenticity unless it is signed. Judging a vane's age only by its appearance is dangerous because aged weather vanes are easy to fake.

Designs made between 1850 and 1925 are highly valued when they can be attributed to such notable manufacturers as J. W. Fiske, Cushing and White, E. G. Washburne & Co., and J. Howard. Since these companies used molds to forge their designs, however, a collector must be aware that many styles were reissued after their original forging and are consequently not as old or valuable as the first issues. Since these second, and even third, forgings can be artificially aged, great caution should be exercised before purchasing a favorite design.

The animal forms that were produced in such great number are generally priced lower than the more exotic shapes, which can sell for thousands of dollars. Fortunately, today, contemporary craftsmen are producing weather vanes for those who cannot afford to pay the high prices demanded by older designs. These new vanes are as meticulously crafted by their creators as the older models, and most of the artists sign, date, and number their creations. In time, these well-crafted weather vanes will become the foundation for future collections, but until then, they can be found pointing into the wind on rooftops throughout the country.

A Day of Sunshine

Henry Wadsworth Longfellow

O gift of God! O perfect day,
Whereon shall no man work, but play,
Whereon it is enough for me,
Not to be doing, but to be!

Through every fibre of my brain,
Through every nerve, through every vein,
I feel the electric thrill, the touch
Of life, that seems almost too much.

I hear the wind among the trees
Playing celestial symphonies;
I see the branches, downward bent,
Like keys of some great instrument.

And over me unrolls on high
The splendid scenery of the sky,
Where through a sapphire sea the sun
Sails like a golden galleon

Toward yonder cloudland in the West,
Toward yonder Islands of the Blest,
Whose steep sierra far uplifts
Its craggy summit white with drifts.

Blow, winds! and waft through all the rooms
The snowflakes of the cherry blooms!
Blow, winds! and bend within my reach
The fiery blossoms of the peach!

O Life and Love! O happy throng
Of thoughts whose only speech is song!
O heart of man! canst thou not be
Blithe as the air is, and as free!

Neighbors

Constance Cullingworth

I watched my neighbor spade and hoe;
I watched him rake and watched him sow
And set new plants out in a row.

I watched him trim and watched him weed
And, here and there, set out a seed
And do the things all gardens need.

I watched him everyday to see
How glad a gardener's work can be;
But I knew not that he watched me.

I looked across the fence last night,
And, oh, it was a lovely sight
With blossoms gold and red and bright!

I saw my neighbor pluck each fair,
New bloom with love and tender care;
I cried when every stalk was bare.

But when I rose at dawn today,
Upon my topmost doorstep lay
A dewy red and gold bouquet.

Photo Opposite
FLORAL SHOWCASE
Near Plainfield, Wisconsin
Ken Dequaine Photography

Remembered Years

May Smith White

Who does not long to go back home again
Where greening hills flow down to meet a stream
And rippling music stirs to life a dream
Half-hidden in the moment's tangled skein?

Forgetting all of fickle youth's disdain,
To lie submerged in magic from the gleam
Of some remembered moon, and trace the scheme
Of rapture, is a power that will sustain.

May I forever hold the ripened years
Against my breast, an ever-shining shield,
Recalling how each treasured hour unlocks
A door that leads beyond the moment's fears.
Who does not long and dare at least to yield
To his desire for home and hollyhocks!

THE PATH AROUND

Douglas Malloch

The path around the house, the way
The common folk use every day,
Near neighbors and the family,
Why, that has always seemed to me
The very best of all to be!

Of course, we have a sidewalk there
In front that's swept and kept with care.
The big front door it leads you to,
And knock, and they will welcome you;
But that's the way that strangers do.

But not "the folks," your very own.
Between the boards, the grass has grown
The front-door way. An endless tide
Keeps smooth and hard and glorified
The little path around the side:

The children laughing with delight
When school lets out; and then at night
Comes Father, weary with the day,
Yet glad to work if only they
Can grow and learn and run and play;

The friends who friends have always been;
The neighbors who have just run in;
And all of those who never need
An invitation first to read
Or any etiquette to heed.

The folks who really love you come
Around the house. It seems that some
Will use the front door to the end;
But, when around the house they wend,
Well, then you know you've got a friend.

The front's for strangers and for style,
The calling card and frozen smile;
The path around is set apart
For folks who aren't proud or smart,
But walk right into house or heart.

This Is Home

Garnett Ann Schultz

I look across these rolling hills
And know that this is home—
The wide expanse of earth and sky
From sweet yesterdays I've known,
The dawning sun which welcomes day
The quiet of the land,
A true blue sky that blesses my way
And helps me understand.

I pause in peacefulness serene
Surveying splendors here:
The trees and hills, the rolling lawn—
Each one is very dear—
The shaded lane where oft I've walked,
The fence that is no more;
The memories now crowd my mind
Of gladness gone before.

So very oft I reminisce
And pause to know again
The grass, all wet with morning dew,
The gentle summer rain.
My heart still overflows with love
For joy that I have known.
Within the stillness, I still dream
And know that this is home.

AN OPPORTUNITY TO COMPLETE YOUR COLLECTION OF IDEALS MAGAZINE!

Here is your once-a-year opportunity to complete your collection of the beautiful and seasonal *Ideals!* Many of our readers request particular issues, but only a few of a limited number of issues are available. Order now, either by phone and credit card, or send us a check at the special price of $3.75 for each book ordered. We will pay postage.

10591A   Valentine   1988
"Sawdust and Dreams" by Edgar A. Guest; Collector's Corner on Old-Fashioned Valentines; directions for making heart sachets and garlands; and "An American Valentine" by Pamela Kennedy.

10621A Summertime   1988
Collector's Corner looks at old postcards; make rose potpourri from backyard roses; "Salute to the Statue of Liberty"; applique a barbecue apron; and gorgeous scenery from around the nation.

10656A   Thanksgiving   1988
"A Time for Settling In" by Carol McCray; applique a Pilgrim potholder; Collector's Corner looks at antique clocks; and Pamela Kennedy's "A Letter Home" from a might-have-been adventurer.

10699A Valentine   1989
Featuring articles on "Phoenix Bird" pattern china; "Down Life's Stream" by Margaret Sangster; craftworks featuring decoupage; and love poetry befitting the season.

10737A   Mother's Day   1989
Norman Rockwell's collectibles are featured; the planting and care of lilacs discussed; "My Cinderella Grandmother" by Kathleen Gilbert; recipes for strawberry torte and other delights.

10788A Christmas   1989
Directions for making felt ornaments for the tree; "A Stable Boy's Christmas" by Pamela Kennedy; "Luke, the Man Who Gave Us Christmas"; "Christmas in America" by Angela Hunt; and "Let Us Keep Christmas" by Grace Noll Crowell.

10826A   Mother's Day   1990
Learn all about "Mothersense," cameos, growing roses, and when nylon stockings were new; travel to "Dixieland," home of Thomas Wolfe, who said, "You can't go home again."

10842A Home   1990
Poems about home, houses, and families; read about gardens and view their beauty; learn how to plant a cutting garden; and collecting antique flatirons.

10869A   Thanksgiving   1990
Poems and prose of Thanksgiving; preparations for winter; photos of nature's autumnal splendor; poems of the harvest; learn about Nathaniel Hawthorne and visit Salem, Massachusetts.

10877A Christmas   1990
Filled with joy, from the story of Christ's birth illustrated with traditional paintings, to how to keep a poinsettia all year, to gifts to make from the kitchen, and beautiful, painted sweatshirts, this is a wonderful issue.

10885A   Valentine   1991
Hummel collectibles; a trip on the *Mississippi Queen* steamboat; Jerome Kern and "Showboat"; "My Mother, My Valentine" by Barbara Smalley; a Valentine door hanging; and sweet Valentine treats.

10907A Mother's Day   1991
Pamela Kennedy's "A Grandmother's Gifts"; directions for making a pretty wallpaper fan; "A Mother's Way" by Edgar A. Guest; a trip to Mackinac Island; Collector's Corner on Victorian lace.

10915A   Country   1991
"Nature" by Thoreau; recipe for hearty oat and wheat bread; the Amana Colonies in Iowa; art by Donald Zolan; collecting antique cookie cutters; "Sonora Smart Dodd: The Mother of Father's Day"; directions for making a braided rag rug.

10923A   Home   1991
Summer flowers and memories of home; directions for decorating a T-shirt or tote bag with a favorite photo; "My Hometown" by Craig E. Sathoff; "Low Maintenance Gardening" by Deana Deck.

10931A Friendship   1991
Eleanor Roosevelt and Louis Howe—a legendary friendship; poetry by Riley, Whittier, Brontë, Stevenson, and others; Crunchy Apple Crisp; directions for drying flowers and making pressed flower bookmarks.

1094XA   Thanksgiving   1991
Jamestown, Virginia, and Pocahontas; "The Oak Leaves" by Edna St. Vincent Millay; "A Gratitude Attitude" by Pamela Kennedy; collecting political buttons; the art of Russ Flint, John Slobodnik, and Patrick McRae.

10958A Christmas   1991
Christmas in Old Salem; recipe for authentic Moravian Molasses Cookies; "Going Home" by Joy Belle Burgess; collecting Madonna Christmas stamps; the story of Christ's birth, illustrated with beautiful stained-glass windows; and read about Legendary American Pearl S. Buck.

10966A   Valentine   1992
Poetry by Edna Jaques, Garnett Ann Schultz, and Grace Noll Crowell and prose by Gladys Taber; visit Niagara Falls; the life of Milton Hershey and recipes for hand-dipped chocolates; collecting antique miniature portraits.

10982A Mother's Day   1992
Beautiful spring floral photographs; make a Mother's Day gift basket; Deana Deck tells how to grow orchids; wonderful recipes for a Mother's Day picnic.

11008A   Country   1992
Grow your own melons to make a delicious cantaloupe swirl cheesecake; a tribute to fathers; John James Audubon and his historic home, Mill Grove; Pamela Kennedy travels "Cross-country."

11016A Home   1992
Gorgeous photographs of homes throughout the country; make your own cross-stitch canning jar lids; Patricia Raybon writes why "Some Things You Keep," and Lansing Christman describes the sights and sounds of summer.

11032A   Thanksgiving   1992
Pamela Kennedy's "Mayflower Journal"; read about Sacajawea, Lewis and Clark's legendary guide, and the community of Taos Pueblo; make a delicious cheddar -chive spoonbread and a hot-dish carrier to hold it.

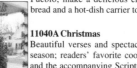
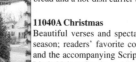

11040A Christmas   1992
Beautiful verses and spectacular photography capture this joyous season; readers' favorite cookie recipes; George Hinke's paintings and the accompanying Scripture celebrate Christ's birth; artwork by Linda Nelson Stocks and Donald Zolan.

To Order:
Please send your name and address, the issue name, date, and number, plus the quantity desired, along with a check or money order for the total amount to:

IDEALS BACK ISSUES
P.O. Box 148000
Nashville, TN 37214-8000

Or Call TOLL FREE 1-800-558-4343
to order by credit card.